A MODERN DAY ZOO

words: Anita Ganeri
consultant: Rob Lovell, Paignton Zoo
illustrations: Toni Hargreaves, Andrew Warrington,
Michéle Dankesreiter, James Stewart

design: Ian Gwilt

RIVERSTON SCHOOL LTD.
63/69 Eltham Road
London
SE12 8UF
Tel: 01-318 4327

British Library Cataloguing in Publication Data
Ganeri, Anita
 A modern zoo.
  1. Zoos. Amphibians. Care
 I. Title II. Hargreaves, Toni III. Warrington, Andrew
 590'.74'4

Copyright © 1990 World International Publishing Limited.
All rights reserved.
Published in Great Britain by World International Publishing Limited,
an Egmont Company, Egmont House, PO Box 111, Great Ducie Street,
Manchester M60 3BL. Printed in Italy. ISBN 0 7235 4298 8

FOREWORD

I'm delighted that a book has been written which goes beyond the daily care of zoo animals and illustrates the fundamental changes that are now taking place in zoos.

We are all aware of the tremendous pressures that threaten animals in the wild, and zoos recognize that they have a special contribution to make to conservation.

As you will discover zoos have long been places of interest and fascination but now they have an increasingly important scientific and educational role. For some species zoos have been the only chance of survival, for many others they are an insurance policy against man's abuse of the living world.

There are a myriad of questions about the how, what and why of a modern zoo. This excellent book knowledgeably provides these answers for the enquiring mind.

*Rob Lovell
Education Officer for
Paignton Zoo*

CONTENTS

Why we have zoos 4
How zoos began 6
Looking after the animals 8
Feeding the animals 10
Where the animals live 12
How a zoo is run 14
Breeding and exchange 16
Studying the animals 18
Success stories 20
Getting involved 24
Learning more about the animals 26
The wild zoos 28
Zoos around the world 30
Glossary 31
Zoo checklist 32

WHY WE HAVE ZOOS

Since they began many years ago, zoos have fascinated people. For most of us, they are the only chance we have of seeing unusual animals from all over the world. When zoos started, their main aim was to entertain people. They were set in pleasant gardens, with animals displayed in small cages. Today zoos have extra, very important jobs to do. Many animals today are in danger of dying out for ever. By the year 2000, a million species may have become extinct. Most of these are small animals but could include large mammals like elephants and rhinos. The main task of most zoos today is to save these animals and educate the public about their plight.

HOW MANY ZOOS?
There are over 750 zoos all around the world. Some 350 million people visit them every year.

DIFFERENT TYPES OF ZOO
Apart from ordinary zoos, there are also hundreds of aquariums, safari parks, game reserves and national parks. Today they are all concerned with providing a safe home for familiar as well as endangered animals.

HOUSING THE ANIMALS
A great deal of thought goes into where the animals live in the zoo. Today, zoos make the animals' enclosures as spacious and natural as possible. This encourages the animals to act naturally and keep happy and healthy.

copyright Chester Zoo

Photo by Rob Lovell, Paignton Zoo

STAR ATTRACTIONS
Zoos work hard encouraging people to visit them. The biggest attractions are very rare animals and baby animals. When the baby polar bear, Brumas, was born in London Zoo in 1949, over 3 million people flocked to see him. Not all zoo animals are as cuddly or interesting but they still need our help.

BREEDING
Zoos used to get all their animals from the wild, through animal dealers. Today most zoo animals are born in zoos. Many endangered species are also being bred in captivity. Some are exchanged for animals from other zoos, or given to them on loan for breeding. A few are released back into the wild, if a safe place can be found for them. This is not always possible because sometimes their wild homes have already been totally destroyed.

CONSERVATION
In the wild, many animals are dying out because their natural home, or habitat, is destroyed. People cut down trees and hedges to make space for building and farming and the animals cannot survive. Zoos try to show people how important it is to save the natural world and the animals in it.

BEHIND THE SCENES
A lot of important work is done behind the scenes at a zoo. Scientists and vets study animal medicine, food and behaviour. Animals are studied in captivity and in the wild. This gives scientists a better idea of how to keep them properly in zoos. It also helps spot problems faced by animals in the wild.

EDUCATION
Zoos can teach us a great deal about animals. They work very hard to make learning fun. Many zoos run classes, lectures and activities to help people understand animals better. Education is an important part of a zoo's work.

Photo by Windsor Safari Park

copyright Chester Zoo

HOW ZOOS BEGAN

People have kept collections of wild animals for thousands of years. This was partly out of curiosity but also because they thought exotic animals were symbols of power. Lions and parrots were often given as gifts to kings and queens. These collections were called menageries. The first public zoos opened in the 1800s. Today we would consider these to be quite cruel places. The animals were kept behind bars in small, dark cages which didn't allow them to behave naturally. Since then zoos have changed in many ways.

CHINESE PARK OF INTELLIGENCE

The Chinese emperors collected and studied animals. In the 1100s BC, Emperor Wen-Wang built a huge 'Park of Intelligence' for his animals. This tradition was carried on by the royal family for hundreds of years. In the 13th century AD, the explorer Marco Polo reported seeing tigers and lions roaming through the royal palace.

ZOOS IN ANCIENT EGYPT

Ancient Egyptian priests kept menageries in their temples over four thousand years ago. The animals included cats, baboons, ibis and lions, which the people worshipped as gods. The Egyptian pharoahs (kings) sent expeditions abroad to find rare animals, such as cheetahs, which they kept for hunting.

ANCIENT GREECE

The Ancient Greeks were among the first people to study the animals they kept. They had many rare and wonderful creatures. In the 4th century BC, Alexander the Great sent back to Greece many animals captured on his travels. They included parrots from India.

ROYAL GIFTS

Gifts of wild animals were seen as much more precious than gold or jewels. When he was crowned in 800 AD, Emperor Charlemagne of France was given a lion from the Pope and an elephant from an Arab ruler. (Today's leaders are also given animals. Queen Elizabeth II has been given jaguars and horses on her travels.)

AZTEC ANIMALS

In about 1520, the Aztec ruler Montezuma had a large 'zoo' at his palace in Tenochtitlan. He kept hawks, eagles, snakes and jaguars. The star attraction, though, was the beautiful quetzal, the sacred bird of the Aztecs.

LONDON ZOO

The word 'zoo' was first used to describe the Zoological Gardens which opened in London in 1827. The zoo was set up with the aim of studying animals and not just using them for entertainment. Since then it has led the way in helping to save rare and endangered animals.

TOWARDS MODERN ZOOS

One of the first modern zoos was Schönbrunn, near Vienna in Austria. It grew out of the menagerie of Emperor Maximilian II who kept wild animals in his royal deer park. The zoo was later opened to the public. In 1828 a giraffe arrived, causing great excitement. People wrote songs about it and held a giraffe festival in its honour. For them the giraffe was as strange as a creature from outer space.

Zoological Society of London

GROWING INTEREST

By the 1870s, there were zoos in many big cities such as Paris, Amsterdam and Frankfurt. Soon they were opened in USA and Australia too. But most of these early zoos put people first. The animals were simply on display for people's enjoyment.

A NEW PART TO PLAY

By the mid 1900s, people became more aware that many wild animals were in danger of dying out forever. In many cases, this was because man was destroying their habitats. So today's zoos have a new part to play – as modern versions of Noah's Ark. They must now try to save whole groups of animals from extinction.

Reproduced by kind permission of Paignton Zoo

LOOKING AFTER THE ANIMALS

Zoos today work very hard to make sure that their animals get the best care possible. Each group of animals has its own keeper who looks after all its needs. Vets visit the animals regularly and treat any who are sick. Large zoos may even have their own animal hospitals.

Photo by Michael Lyster, London Zoo

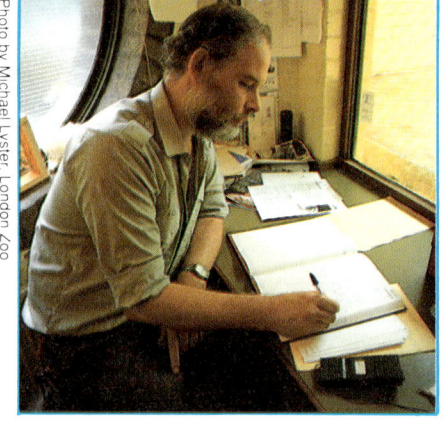

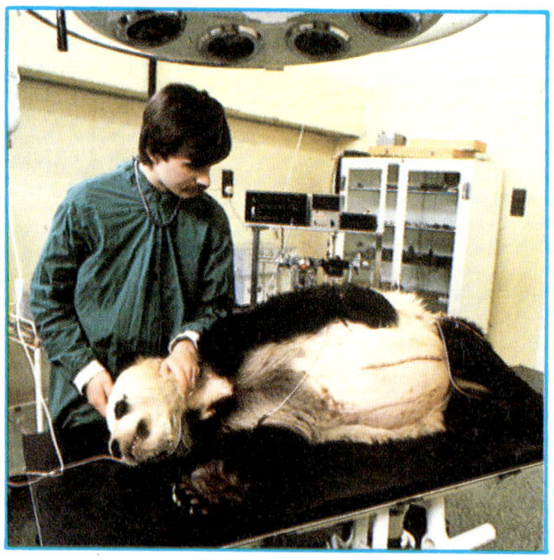

Photo by Michael Lyster, London Zoo

THE KEEPER

The keeper has to feed the animals, clean them out and check that they are healthy and happy. If there are any problems, he discusses them with the head keeper or the vet. Often zoos allow keepers to work with the animals that interest them most. Keepers study their animals carefully and exchange information with zoos all over the world. They also get involved in animal breeding programmes.

THE VET

The vet is an animal doctor who treats sick animals and also makes sure that healthy animals stay healthy. For example, zebra and Barbary sheep have their hooves trimmed every year. Otherwise they can become overgrown and stop the animals standing and walking properly. The vet also repairs bite or peck wounds and gives animals regular vaccinations to prevent diseases.

LONGER LIVES

Because they are well looked after, many zoo animals live longer than they would in the wild. The normal lifespan for a wild lion is 12–14 years, but the oldest zoo lion reached the grand old age of about 29. His name was Nero and he lived in Cologne Zoo, West Germany.

SPECIAL RELATIONSHIP

Where possible, zoos encourage animals to behave as they would in the wild, and not become tame. But some animals form close bonds with their keepers. At Hamburg Zoo, people are allowed to pass fruit over the moat to the elephants. Unfortunately, some people give the elephants coins instead, which can harm them. To avoid this the keepers train the elephants to hand the coins to them in return for a treat.

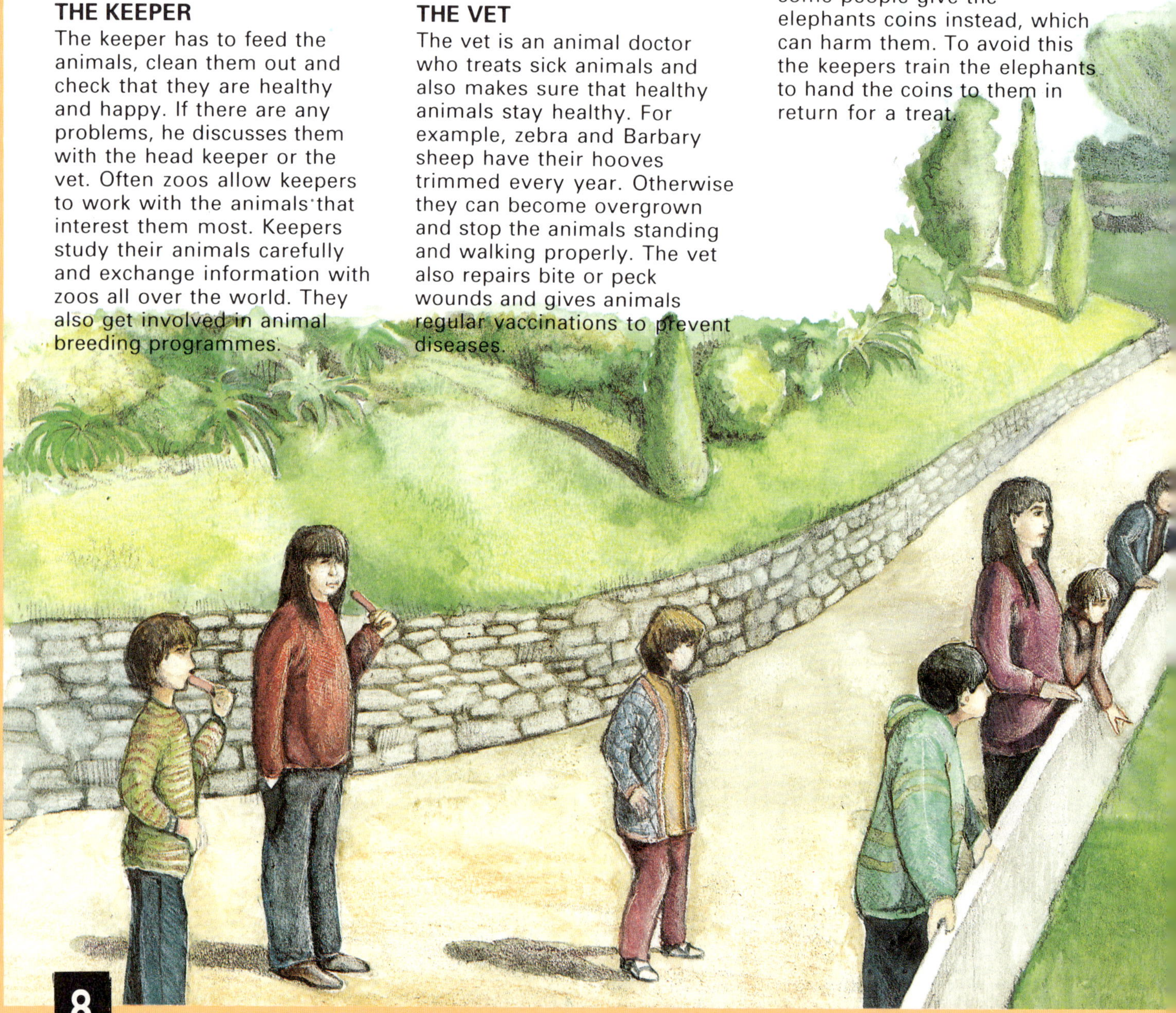

TRAINING FOR ZOO WORK
Keepers have to know a lot about the animals' needs and behaviour. They attend special courses to learn about caring for animals and how to detect problems. Keepers also have to be physically fit and prepared to work in all weathers. Most of all they need to be reliable and have real concern for their animals.

MODERN EQUIPMENT
The vet may use modern hospital equipment to examine and treat the animals. He may use a lapiscope (a slim instrument with a light at the end) to look inside birds to see if they are male or female. Often with birds you can't see the difference from the outside.

ANIMAL ILLNESSES
Some animals, like gorillas, suffer from coughs, colds and tummy upsets just as people do. Part of a vet's work is to treat these common illnesses. Another part is treating and trying to prevent more serious diseases, such as measles. The vet may also be called to treat tapirs with abscesses on their faces and penguins with lung infections which make them lose their appetites.

IN THE ANIMAL HOSPITAL
Most sick animals are best treated in their enclosures. Some drugs are now given by dart from a blow pipe. If an animal is very ill, it might be taken to the hospital for an operation. The animal is given an anaesthetic so the vet can treat it without putting it under any stress. A broken bone may have to be set and the patient kept quiet until it mends. In Chicago Zoo, a middle-aged gorilla with arthritis even had a hip replaced to help her walk again.

copyright Chester Zoo

FEEDING THE ANIMALS

All the animals in a zoo have their food carefully planned and prepared. A balanced diet should include all the vitamins and minerals needed to keep the animals healthy. It should also be as much like the animals' natural diet as possible. Zoos study the animals' feeding times and habits in the wild and try to copy them. Big cats, for example, do not catch food every day in the wild, so in the zoo they go for two days a week without being fed. They also have special diets for babies, pregnant mothers and sick animals.

FLAMINGO FOOD
In the wild, flamingoes use their special beaks to filter algae and tiny shrimps out of the water. These contain a pigment (colouring) called carotene which makes the flamingoes' feathers pink. In zoos, carotene is added to their food. Otherwise their feathers would fade and they would not breed well.

ELEPHANT APPETITE
Elephants are the largest living land animals and need an enormous amount of food. They are herbivores (plant-eaters) and in the wild eat about 180kg of plants and leaves a day. Their zoo diet is richer, so they don't need to eat as much. But an Asian elephant still manages to munch about 45kg of vegetables, hay and grass pellets a day. A zoo spends about £7,000 a year on food for an elephant.

CHALLENGE FOR THE CHIMPS
Zurich Zoo encourages its chimps to feed using their natural skills. In the wild, chimps poke twigs inside termite mounds and pull out termites to eat. In Zurich, the chimps have artificial termite mounds filled with mashed fruit and honey. A plentiful supply of twigs lies nearby. This makes life more interesting for the chimps.

SEA OTTER SUPPER
Zoo sea otters are quite happy with a diet of fish. But at Seattle Aquarium, USA, the keeper empties a bucket of clams into the otter pool, together with a pile of stones. The sea otter balances a stone on its stomach and smashes the clams open on it – just as it would in the wild.

FEEDING THE SNAKES
Snakes such as boas and pythons are fed once a week with whole rats or mice. In the wild, snakes often go for a long time without eating, especially during mating and when they are shedding their skins. After its fast, a large snake may eat up to ten rats in one go.

HAND-REARING BABIES
Sometimes the parents of birds such as parrots reject their babies and won't feed them. Then their keeper has to feed them special liquid food through a syringe or pipette. Most hand-reared animals would not do well in the wild, though, because they don't learn natural behaviour and skills from their parents.

BUSHBABIES
The keepers make sure that the animals' food is always fresh. Bushbabies are given fruit salad, with chopped apples, grapes, nuts, bananas and added vitamins. For dessert, they have a bowl of meal worms.

EATING IN PUBLIC
In most zoos, people can watch the penguins being fed. They usually have two meals a day of herrings and multi-vitamins. A penguin eats about eight herrings a day. Before it moults (loses its old feathers) though, it may eat about three times this much and then stop eating for about two weeks. Penguins moult once a year.

WHERE THE ANIMALS LIVE

The first animal enclosures were built to give people the best view of the animals. The cages had strong iron bars and were rather like prison cells. Today moats, glass and electric fencing are used to separate the animals from the public. Zoos are now working towards building natural enclosures, based on the animals' needs. For the animals to behave naturally, they need space to move about and plenty to interest them. They also need safe places to retreat to when escaping from fights or for breeding.

GETTING RID OF THE BARS
One man who worked hard to change the way animals were kept was a German, Carl Hagenbeck. In the early 1900s he bought some land near Hamburg and set up his own zoo. His animals were not kept behind bars, though. His were among the first large enclosures with moats. Many zoos soon followed his example.

MOONLIT WORLD
Nocturnal animals are active during the night. Many large zoos have nocturnal houses where day and night are reversed so you can see the animals feeding and grooming. Special lighting is used to look like moonlight so you can watch mole rats, fennec foxes, lorises and fruit bats.

HONEY BEARS
In Copenhagen Zoo, Denmark, a lot of thought has been given to the bear enclosure. To show how well bears climb, it has an amazing tree. Honey is pumped up through the trunk and the bears can climb up and enjoy a treat. In the wild the bears would raid bees' nests up in the trees.

CHIMPS AT PLAY
In the wild, chimpanzees live in large family groups. They are very sociable and love playing and climbing. At Taronga Zoo in Sydney, Australia this need has been recognized. The chimps have a large, grassy enclosure with a stream, rocks and trees. They play and romp as they would in the wild.

REPTILE HOUSE
Most reptiles come from warm places. Being cold-blooded they need to keep warm so their bodies work properly. Zoos keep their reptile houses well heated at about 26°–29°C so that the snakes, lizards and crocodiles are comfortable.

LIVING TOGETHER
Some zoos group animals together as they would be in the wild. Toronto Zoo in Canada has four pavilions, each showing a different part of the world. In the African pavilion there are muddy swamps and a lush jungle, with many African plants such as palm and banana trees. Mandrills, gorillas, pythons and buffaloes are kept apart in special cages which blend in with the landscape.

CLIMB WITH THE GORILLAS
Jersey Zoo's famous gorillas live in a large enclosure. It has a huge mound covered with long grass, some dead trees and a small pool. There are also trees with ropes for the gorillas to climb up. Outside the enclosure is a climbing frame for children with a sign on it saying 'gorillas like watching kids climb'!

Photo by Philip Coffey, Jersey Wildlife Preservation Trust

AQUARIUMS
Aquariums filled with brightly-coloured tropical fish are always popular. Zoos make their own seawater by adding chemicals to fresh water. The water is kept clean and at the right temperature with the help of filters and even computers.

RAIN EVERY HOUR
Chicago Zoo's spectacular Tropic World is as big as two football pitches and is the largest zoo building in the world. Three huge halls house animals from South America, Asia and Africa. Every hour there is the sound of thunder and a tropical rainstorm showers down from sprinklers in the roof.

HOW A ZOO IS RUN

Behind the scenes there is a whole team of people who make a zoo run smoothly. Some care for the animals; others make the zoo attractive to visitors. In some countries, zoos get money from their government to help pay their bills. In Britain, most large zoos are run as charities. This means that they rely solely on visitors' money, and sometimes donations, to keep going. Zoos around the world are all run slightly differently but these pages give a general idea of the people involved in a large zoo.

THE BOARD OF DIRECTORS OR TRUSTEES
These are people who have special knowledge which can help the zoo. They might include scientists, bankers and solicitors. They advise the executive director on what they think the zoo should be doing.

THE EXECUTIVE DIRECTOR
The job of the executive director is to get people in the zoo to carry out the board of directors' plans. These might include building a new enclosure, improving the signs around the zoo or running special publicity events.

THE CURATOR
The person in charge of the animal side of the zoo is called the curator. Below him or her come the head keepers and keepers who look after the different groups of animals, such as the mammals or reptiles. Each group may be further divided into individual species, such as lions, gorillas or lizards.

RESEARCH
Large zoos often have their own research department. They have laboratories where zoologists do work on diet, breeding and so on. They also keep detailed records of all the zoo's animals. Vets work on research into animal illnesses and possible cures.

GARDENERS AND GROUNDSTAFF

Great care is taken to make zoos pleasant places to visit. The gardens are kept well-stocked and well looked after. Some zoos grow their own food for the animals, for example, leafy branches for elephants and giraffe to browse on. The groundstaff and maintenance staff also keep the cages and enclosures in good repair.

SHOPS AND CAFÉS

Most zoos have souvenir shops where you can buy books, gifts and postcards. There are also staff to run restaurants and cafés for hungry visitors.

EDUCATION DEPARTMENT

An important part of a zoo's work is to teach people more about animals and help them understand them better. Many zoos have their own education departments. They organize school visits, lectures and activities. They may also produce information booklets and worksheets for teachers, pupils and the general public.

VOLUNTEERS

People who live locally and are interested in animals can sometimes work as volunteers. They do a wide range of tasks, from gardening to guiding small groups of visitors round the zoo. Volunteers are always welcome and it is an enjoyable way to help conservation.

ZOOS WORKING TOGETHER

Good zoos know that they have to work together to do their job well. In most countries, people from different zoos meet regularly to discuss breeding, scientific study and research. There is also an International Union of Zoo Directors where zoo directors from all over the world meet to discuss their ideas.

Paignton Zoo seen from the air.

Reproduced by kind permission of Paignton Zoo

BREEDING AND EXCHANGE

A zoo's most important job today is the conservation (saving) of endangered animals. Many animals are on the brink of becoming extinct, through hunting or as their wild habitats are destroyed. For some, zoos are the only safe places left. Many zoos encourage their rare animals to breed and some are eventually released back into the wild. Other animals would no longer be safe in their wild homes and zoos must try to keep them successfully in captivity so they do not become extinct.

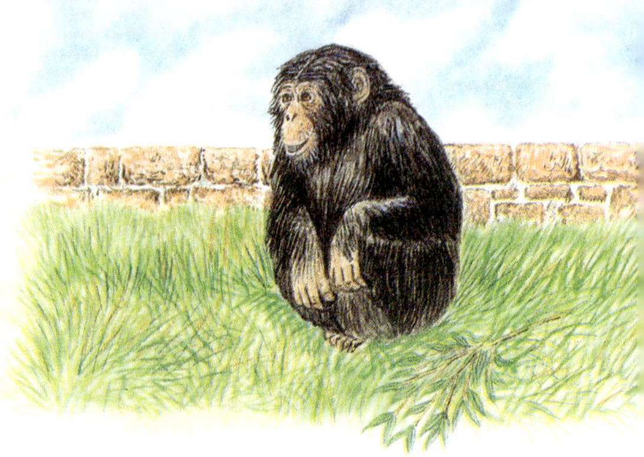

ALL CHANGE

Zoos often lend their animals to other zoos for breeding. The giant panda is the symbol of the World Wide Fund for Nature and an endangered animal. London Zoo have lent their panda, Chia Chia, to Chapultatec Zoo in Mexico. They hope he will mate with the zoo's female panda, one of seven pandas already born at the zoo.

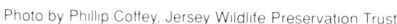

Photo by Phillip Coffey, Jersey Wildlife Preservation Trust

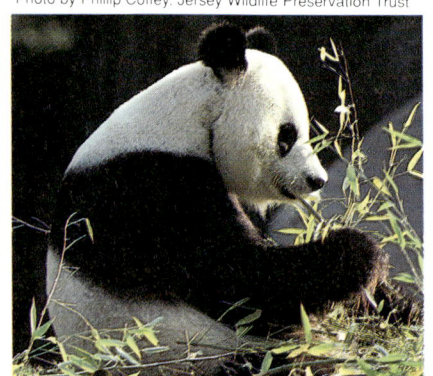

NO TRAPPING

Most zoo animals today are born in zoos and no longer have to be taken from the wild. In the past, trappers were paid large sums of money to catch animals for private collections, medical research, pets and for zoos. They killed whole groups of chimps, for example, to get one baby, which often died on the way to the zoo.

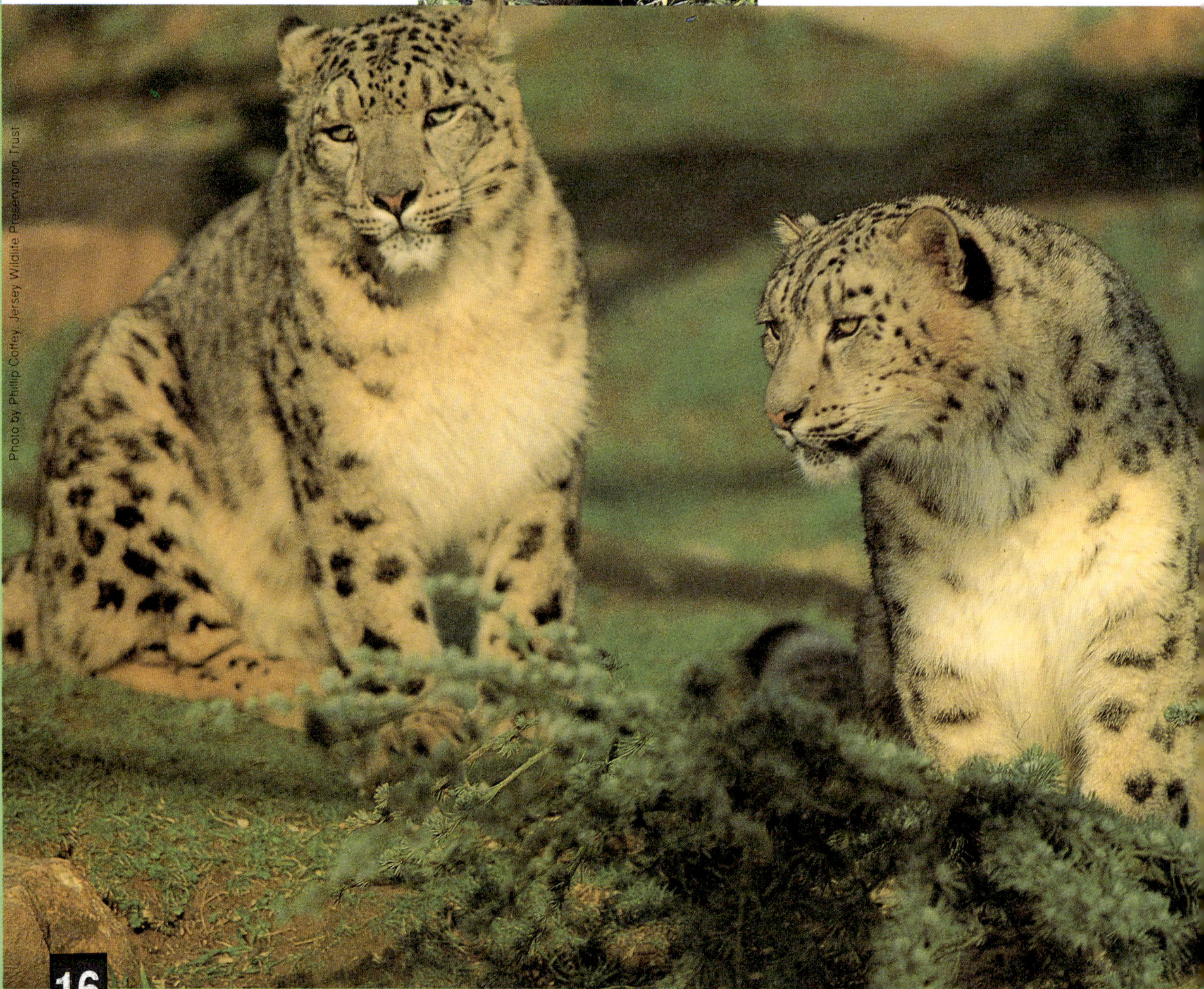

Photo by Phillip Coffey, Jersey Wildlife Preservation Trust

BREEDING CENTRES

Some zoos have separate breeding centres which are closed to the public. New York Zoo has its breeding centre on a small island off the coast of Georgia. Here they breed oryx, tortoises and many other animals. These may be released back into the wild or sent to supply other zoos.

TRAVELLING ABROAD

When zoos send their animals abroad, they make careful travel arrangements. The animals often travel by plane to cut down the length of the journey. Some, like rhinoceroses, have to be given tranquilizers so they can be put into their crates safely and to reduce the stress of being handled.

IN PRIVATE

Some animals will only mate if the conditions are right and similar to those in the wild. Congo peafowl, for example, are quite nervous, shy birds and only breed well if they have privacy.

LOST FOR EVER

In the days before zoos fully understood how they could save animals by captive breeding, some animals died out whilst in captivity. The last quagga (a type of zebra) died in Amsterdam Zoo in 1883. They were already extinct in the wild. Passenger pigeons were once the commonest birds in North America, but in 1914 the last pigeon died in Cincinnati Zoo.

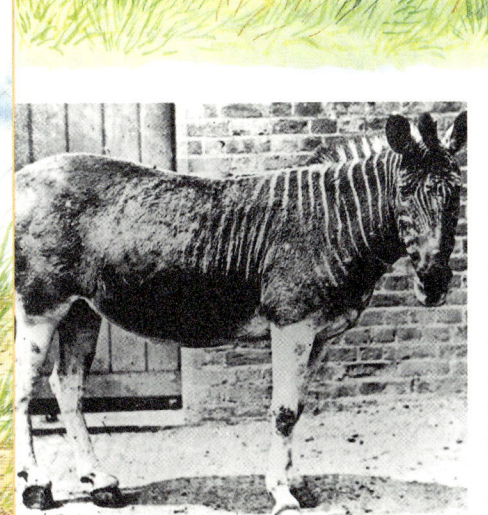
Zoological Society of London

WORLD FIRST

Because of the research done into breeding, zoos have had great successes. On 17 April 1961 the first male zoo-bred gorilla was born in Basle Zoo, Switzerland. His name is Jambo and he now lives in Jersey Zoo. By 1988 he had been a father 18 times and his babies are now growing up in zoos all over the USA and Europe.

Photo by Phillip Coffey. Jersey Wildlife Preservation Trust

KEEPING RECORDS

Zoos keep detailed records of all their animals. Studbooks give details about an animal's parents and breeding success. If other zoos need a particular animal they can look it up quickly in these books. Zoos often put their records on computer and there is an international computer network so zoos can exchange information quickly.

STUDYING THE ANIMALS

Scientists only have detailed information about 40 species of animals. Most of them are farm animals, such as cows and sheep. Zoos give scientists a wonderful opportunity to study wild animals from all over the world. They study the animals' feeding and breeding habits, illnesses and their general behaviour. All this helps zoos to keep animals successfully in captivity, and to release some back into the wild. Large zoos often have their own laboratories where zoologists work.

FOOD STUDIES

Some of the research done into what animals eat is used to save animals in the wild. In Africa baby elephants are sometimes left as orphans when their parents are shot by poachers. Scientists can feed the babies on liquid food made up to contain all the goodness of a mother elephant's milk. Zoos use computers to help them study diets.

CHEETAH CARE

A great deal of research goes into creating the ideal breeding conditions for zoo animals. Whipsnade Zoo in Britain found that their cheetahs would only breed if the males and females stayed apart until they were ready to mate, as they would in the wild. Since then over 100 cubs have been born at Whipsnade.

FIELD WORK

Zoos send scientists abroad to study animals in the wild. This gives them a better idea of how the animals behave naturally and helps when it comes to planning enclosures and diets in the zoo. A team from London Zoo was sent to study the endangered black rhino in Kenya. They learned the age and sex of the animals from their footprints.

Photo by David Jones, London Zoo

Photo by Terry Dennett, London Zoo

CHECKING PROGRESS
When animals are released back into the wild, a careful eye is kept on their progress. Often animals are fitted with radio collars or radio ear tags so that researchers can keep in close contact with them. They can make sure the animals are eating properly and not straying outside the safety of their reserve.

TRAINING CENTRES
Some zoos, such as Jersey Zoo, have special centres where they train students from all over the world. They learn how to look after endangered species in their own countries through lectures, projects and observing and working with the zoo's animals.

NATURAL BEHAVIOUR
Research done in the wild helps zoos find ways of designing enclosures so animals behave naturally in captivity. In the wild, gorillas spend a lot of their time browsing for leaves or foraging for food on the forest floor. In the zoo, they are given regular meals but also given the chance to find food for themselves.

HELP FOR HUMANS
A lot of medical research is done in zoos. Sometimes this may be used to help humans too. Scientists have found that the bacteria which causes the terrible disease leprosy can be grown in armadillos. It does not harm the animals and scientists can then test drugs for treating leprosy on the armadillos.

USING COMPUTERS
Computers are very important for sorting information. When closely related animals breed, their babies are often unhealthy and may not live long. To avoid this, zoos exchange information about their animals by computer. They can then help each other to produce healthy animals.

19

SUCCESS STORIES

When zoos release zoo-born animals back into the wild, it is called reintroduction. It takes years of careful planning before this can happen. First of all, the zoo's own captive breeding programme has to have good results. A safe place in the wild then has to be chosen where the animals will have enough food and be able to breed. On the next few pages you can read about some of the success stories so far.

PRZEWALSKI'S HORSE

When this wild horse was discovered in 1881 by Colonel N. M. Przewalski, a Polish cavalry officer, large herds were still found in Mongolia. By 1945 there were less than 100 horses left in the wild. Zoos started with a group of ten horses and by 1981 the world herd was over 400 strong. In recent years large numbers have been reintroduced into Mongolia where they compete for grazing land with the wild Przewalski's horse.

HAWAIIAN GOOSE

In the 18th century there were about 25,000 Hawaiian geese, or ne-ne, living on the slopes of Hawaii's volcanoes. But people who came to live on the islands hunted them for food and the settlers' mongooses and cats ate their eggs and goslings. By 1952 there were only about 30 birds left. Zoos and reserves, in particular the Wildfowl Trust, came to the rescue, and in 1978 released 1,600 birds back into the wild.

PÈRE DAVID'S DEER

Père David's deer lived in the marshy swamps of China. In 1865 a French missionary, Père David, saw some deer in the Chinese Emperor's garden. They had probably already been extinct in the wild for hundreds of years. Zoos took some animals and built up a world herd of about 1000 animals. In 1986, 39 deer were returned to the wild, in a special reserve in China.

ARABIAN ORYX
In 1982, 14 zoo-bred Arabian oryx were released into the wild in Oman. They are closely guarded. These beautiful animals had been hunted for their skin and meat and by 1972 there were none left in the wild. In 1962 Phoenix Zoo, Arizona, USA started a world herd with three oryx. It is now over 300 strong.

PARTULA SNAILS
Mammals and birds are not the only animals in danger. The tiny partula snail is now extinct in its natural island home of Moorea Atoll in the South Pacific Ocean. Several zoos are now involved in breeding these tiny creatures. Captive breeding need not be very expensive. A container the size of a shoe-box can be used for these snails.

GOLDEN LION TAMARIN
This tiny monkey was thought to be the world's most endangered mammal. Its home in the Brazilian rain forest was cut down and babies were taken by animal traders. The National Zoo in Washington, USA, set up an international programme to save the tamarin from extinction. In 1987 a group of 15 was released into a protected reserve in Brazil.

PINK PIGEON
In 1978 only about 30 pink pigeons were left on the island of Mauritius, in the Indian Ocean. People cut down trees in their forest home and monkeys raided their nests. Some birds were taken to Jersey Zoo where they bred well. In 1987 eleven pigeons were released into the wild.

CALIFORNIAN CONDOR
At one time, it was thought that at most only 20 of these magnificent birds survived in the wild. The first chick ever born in captivity hatched at San Diego Zoo, USA. So that the chick learnt to behave normally, its keepers used a leather puppet shaped like a condor head to feed the baby. They also played tapes of the sounds parent birds make while chicks are hatching in the wild.

DEAD AS A DODO
Thanks to breeding successes, many animals have been saved from the brink of extinction. The flightless dodo of Mauritius was less lucky. European explorers first discovered the dodo in 1599 but only a hundred years later it had been hunted to extinction.

ROUND ISLAND BOA
Round Island lies off the coast of Mauritius. It is home to the world's rarest snake – a type of boa. In 1977 Jersey Zoo collected the first Round Island boa to be kept in captivity. After years of hard work, the first boa eggs hatched in 1985. Forceps were used to feed the tiny thread-like babies with meat.

CHOOSING THE SITE
Before animals are released into the wild, zoos spend a lot of time negotiating with the government of the country involved and local conservation groups to make sure the animals will be well protected. Then they monitor the animals for months or years afterwards to see that they are settling in.

SUCCESS STORIES

SNOW LEOPARD
The snow leopard, or ounce, is one of the most beautiful big cats. It is a very secretive animal and rarely seen in its wild mountain home. The leopard has long been hunted for its fur and is in great danger. Zoos all over the world, in Switzerland and the USA, for example, are now involved in breeding programmes to save the snow leopard.

RADIATED TORTOISE
If they can feed and breed in safety, tortoises can live for up to 200 years. But they are killed in huge numbers for their meat and beautiful shells, and captured for pets. The radiated tortoise is now officially protected in Madagascar and trading in tortoises is forbidden. With the help of conservation groups and zoos, it is hoped that they will breed and increase their numbers.

INSTINCT FOR SURVIVAL
If animals lose their natural instincts for survival, such as finding food and escaping from danger, they will not last long in the wild. By encouraging their animals to behave as naturally as possible in captivity, zoos make sure they stand a good chance of surviving in the wild.

GETTING INVOLVED

Another important part of a zoo staff's work is to make people more familiar with the animals in their care. They hope that if people understand the animals better they will do more to try and save them. Zoos have many ways of getting people involved and making zoo visits both interesting and fun.

CHIMPS' TEA PARTIES
Until 1972 London Zoo held chimps' tea parties, which were very popular. But as more research was done into how animals behaved naturally, the parties were stopped. Although the chimps seemed to enjoy playing, they often found it difficult to settle back into their groups afterwards. Today, zoos may put on bird of prey displays which don't make fun of the animals, but encourage natural behaviour.

ADOPT AN ANIMAL
Many zoos run schemes for adopting animals, from ants to rhinoceroses. People pay to adopt a whole, small animal or part of a larger animal. The money goes towards the animal's food and general care. You receive a certificate, a photo, and a plaque with your name on it is displayed on the animal's cage. Some schools adopt a zoo animal.

MOBILE ZOO
Philadelphia Zoo in the USA takes the zoo out to the people. A van is equipped with cages and the keepers take the animals to schools, old people's homes and so on.

SHARING THE ANIMALS' WORLD
Enclosures are often designed so that people feel part of the animals' world. At Sea World, Florida, USA, the giant shark tanks are a thrilling experience. You stand on a moving walkway and go through a tunnel with sharks swimming all around you. It is quite safe, though. You are separated from the sharks by a thick pane of tough acrylic.

EDUCATION

A zoo's education department works hard to make learning about animals fun. It works with groups of all ages, from playschool children to university students, as well as general visitors. The education department prepares talks and interesting activity classes where you may be able to handle skulls, horns, feathers – and even live animals.

ACTIVITY CENTRES

Paignton Zoo in Devon was the first zoo in Great Britain to develop a family activity centre. Here you can race on bicycles to see if you can go faster than an ostrich or a cheetah. There is a giant spider's web to climb on, computers to play with, brass rubbing, and much more.

ZOO SCHOOL

Cincinnati Zoo, USA, even has its own school within the zoo. Here pupils study all the usual school subjects but also learn about keeping zoo animals. Many go on to become vets, zoo keepers or zoologists.

Photo by Rob Lovell, Paignton Zoo

Photo by Peter Stevens, Paignton Zoo

CHILDREN'S ZOO

In children's zoos there are familiar animals, such as pigs, sheep and goats, together with more unusual creatures, such as llamas. You can see the animals close up and even stroke and handle them. Copenhagen Zoo has a superb rabbit maze. You pretend to be a rabbit and escape from enemies like foxes and buzzards by diving down slides into an underground warren.

YOU IN THE ZOO

Seeing animals close to is very exciting but you must always treat them carefully. Remember that tapping or banging on their cages frightens the animals. Never be tempted to feed them, especially with crisp packets, chewing gum, pencils and coins. These can injure the animals very badly, or even kill them.

LEARNING MORE ABOUT THE ANIMALS

By wandering around a zoo and watching the animals, you can learn a great deal about them. You can find out how they behave, how they feed, what noises they make and how they move. Look out for the signs on the animals' cages. These give information about where animals come from, which animal family they belong to, how they live in the wild, and so on. Here you can see what a typical sign looks like. Use the information on the next page to make up your own signs.

SPECIAL FEATURES
Many animals have special or unusual features. Giraffes are the tallest animals on earth. An adult male stands nearly 6 metres tall. A staggering 2 metres of this is neck!

Photo by Rob Lovell, Paignton Zoo

Photo by Jo Unwin, Paignton Zoo

THE GIRAFFE'S PROPER NAME
The sign on the giraffe house shows a picture of the animal with its scientific, Latin name, *Giraffa camelopardalis*. Scientific names are used to avoid confusion. Common names for animals differ from country to country but the same scientific name is used all over the world.

FAMILY NAME
Animals are divided into large groups called classes, then into smaller groups called orders. The giraffe belongs to the class of mammals and to the order of even-toed ungulates. These names may also appear on the zoo signs.

NATURAL HOME
A map shows you where the animals come from. Giraffes live in the dry, grassy plains of Africa, to the south of the Sahara Desert.

DIET AND BEHAVIOUR
Other information on the sign may tell you what the animals eat, how they behave and when they have babies. In the wild, giraffes browse on leaves high up in thorny acacia trees. In the zoo, they eat hay, leaves, chopped vegetables and extra vitamins.

AMERICAN ALLIGATOR
The American alligator *(Alligator mississippiendis)* lives in the marshy swamps of North America. In the zoo, alligators eat fish, rats and meat, three times a week. Alligators mate in water and the female lays about 40 eggs at a time. The newly-hatched babies are about 30cm long.

EMU
Emus *(Dromaius novaehollandiae)* live in small flocks in Australia. Their wild diet consists of insects and berries; in the zoo they eat fruit and vegetables. The females lay dark green eggs and the chicks are white with yellow and black stripes. Emus cannot fly but they are fast runners.

MEXICAN RED-KNEED TARANTULA
This spider *(Brachypelma smithi)* is now endangered in Mexico because so many spiders have been collected for pets. In the wild, the spiders eat insects, reptiles and birds. They are often called bird-eating spiders. Unlike other spiders, tarantulas do not spin webs, but hunt for prey.

TIGER
Tigers *(Panthera tigris)* once lived all over Asia, Malaysia and Indonesia in long grass and forests. Today, Bali and Caspian tigers are probably extinct and the other six species are endangered. In zoos tigers eat joints of meat, rabbits and chickens. They don't eat for one or two days a week, as they would not eat every day in the wild.

RODRIGUES FRUIT BAT
These bats *(Pteropus rodricensis)* live in the forest on the tiny island of Rodrigues, near Mauritius. They are now very rare because almost all their forest home has been cut down. The bats feed at night on mangoes, lychees and flowers. In the zoo, they eat all sorts of fruit. During the day they hang upside-down on branches, grooming and resting. Bats are the only mammals that can truly fly.

THE WILD ZOOS

The best way to see wild animals is in their natural habitat, but most of us don't have the time or money to make this possible. Sometimes there is no natural habitat left. All over the world, forests and grasslands are being destroyed and rivers and seas polluted by spilt oil and chemicals. Many countries have, therefore, set aside large areas where animals and plants can live safely in their natural homes. These are called national parks. The animals here are protected, which means it is against the law to catch or kill them.

OPEN ZOOS

National parks are like huge open zoos because they still have to manage their animals carefully. For example, tiger reserves in India have special buffer zones to keep the tigers away from the farmers' animals. In the USA, wolves used to be removed from some reserves so they did not kill the deer. But this meant that the deer population grew too quickly and destroyed the plant life. National parks must maintain the natural balance.

YELLOWSTONE NATIONAL PARK

Yellowstone National Park in the USA was the world's first national park and is the largest in the USA. It was set up in 1872 and today covers over 800,000 hectares. The park's most famous animals are grizzly bears and bison. Both have been saved from extinction by the safety of the park.

RAIN FOREST PARK

Each year huge areas of tropical rain forest are cut down and burned. This means disaster for hundreds of kinds of animals. The Parque Nacional da Amazonia is 10,000 square kilometres of protected rain forest along the Amazon river in Brazil. Here armadillos, giant anteaters, toucans and frogs can live safely.

SERENGETI NATIONAL PARK

Many African countries have national parks. These are the only places where elephants, for example, can still be seen in the wild. Here they are protected from poachers who kill them for their ivory tusks. The Serengeti National Park covers nearly 15,000 square kilometres of grassland in Tanzania, East Africa. It is famous for its great herds of gnu, gazelles and zebras.

TURTLE BEACH

Mon Repos Beach in Queensland, Australia, offers another way of watching animals. Turtles, such as endangered loggerhead turtles, come to this sandy beach to lay their eggs. The females haul themselves out of the sea and dig nests with their flippers. They lay their eggs and cover them with sand. You can watch but are not allowed to talk or move until the eggs have been laid.

TREETOPS

Treetops is a famous place in Kenya where people can go and watch wildlife. It is like a hotel on stilts, built around a water hole. In the evening buffaloes, storks, wart-hogs and even rhinos come to drink right in front of visitors' eyes. Baboons too invade the viewing terrace in search of food.

SAVE THE PANDA

Giant pandas were once a common sight in China. But today there are only about 500 left in the wild. Pandas live on bamboo. If this is cut down or dies out, the pandas starve. In 1981 a campaign to save the panda was launched and they are now strictly protected in special reserves in south-west China.

LOCAL NATURE RESERVES

National parks protect wildlife on a very grand scale. But local nature reserves are an important part of conservation too, and something anyone can help with. Waste land is often used by wild animals and needs to be looked after. Local people in north London have turned a disused railway line into a city nature reserve.

KAZIRANGE NATIONAL PARK

This park covers a large area of flat, swampy land on the banks of the Brahmaputra river in Assam, India. It is famous for its rhinos and swamp deer. It is also home to leopards, herons, eagles and tigers, which were once common in this part of the world.

ZOOS AROUND THE WORLD

Today there are hundreds of zoos all over the world. Some began by accident, whilst others were the result of years of hard work by animal lovers. Not all zoos live up to the high standards set by large zoos such as London or New York, but most take their task of saving endangered animals very seriously. Here you can read about some of the world's best and most famous zoos.

FRANKFURT ZOO

Frankfurt Zoo opened in 1858. During World War II it was nearly destroyed and about ninety per cent of its animals killed. It was soon being rebuilt and putting new ideas about animal enclosures into practice. The Bird House was the first where the birds could fly about freely. The only gorilla twins ever known were born at Frankfurt Zoo.

JERSEY ZOO

Jersey Zoo specializes in keeping endangered animals. It was started by the author, Gerald Durrell, in 1959 and is now part of the Jersey Wildlife Preservation Trust. The Trust has studied and bred many endangered animals, such as white-eared pheasants and volcano rabbits. It shares its animals with zoos all over the world and also releases some back into the wild.

PEKING ZOO

There have been zoos in China for thousands of years, but Peking Zoo did not open to the public until the 1950s. Today it is famous for its giant pandas. The first pandas arrived in 1955 when people realized that they needed to study them to save them from extinction. In 1963 the zoo had the first panda cub born in captivity. The baby was called Ming Ming.

METRO TORONTO ZOO

Toronto Zoo opened in 1974 and was the first zoo to group its animals together as they would be in the wild. A train ride will take you through Africa, Asia, North and South America and Australia. Toronto is very cold in winter so animals from tropical climates have well-heated dens indoors.

SAN DIEGO ZOO

San Diego Zoo is one of the largest zoos in the world. It is famous for its research and conservation work. Among many other successes, it has helped set up a conservation programme for the lemurs of Madagascar. San Diego is one of the only zoos outside Australia that keeps koalas. This is because San Diego has sunshine nearly all year round, so the zoo can grow enough eucalyptus to keep the animals well fed.

copyright Peter Wait, Senior Curator, Chester Zoo

GLOSSARY

captive breeding – the breeding of animals in zoos.

class – the large group to which similar animals belong, such as mammal, reptile, bird.

cold-blooded – animals, such as lizards, that cannot control their own body temperature and rely on warm weather to be active.

conservation – protecting and helping to save wildlife.

endangered – animals that are in danger of dying out forever (becoming extinct).

extinct – animals that have died out and no longer exist. If there have been no records of an animal for 50 years it is declared to be extinct, for example, the dodo, and dinosaurs.

field work – the study of animals in their wild, natural homes.

habitat – the type of place where an animal lives, such as forest, grassland, desert.

herbivore – an animal that eats mainly or only plants, such as an elephant.

marsupial – mammals with pouches, such as kangaroos and koalas. Their new-born babies are tiny, and crawl into the mother's pouch to feed and grow.

menagerie – an early collection of wild animals, often owned by a country's rulers.

monotremes – mammals which lay eggs, such as duck-billed platypuses.

national park – a large area of wild countryside where animals can live safely in their natural surroundings.

nocturnal – animals that rest during the day and are active at night, such as fennec foxes and bats.

order – a smaller group to which an animal belongs. For example, gorillas belong to the primate order and tigers to the carnivore order.

protected – rare or endangered animals are often protected. This means it is against the law to catch or kill them.

reintroduction – releasing animals born in a zoo back into a safe, natural home in the wild.

species – a group of animals that are very similar and can breed successfully.

warm-blooded – animals which can control their own body temperature, so they can be active in heat or cold.

world herd – the world herd of Arabian oryx, for example, includes all the Arabian oryx in zoos all over the world.

zoo-bred – animals that are born in zoos.

zoologist – a scientist who studies animals.

zoological gardens – the original name for a zoo. The word zoo is a shortened version of zoological gardens.

ZOO CHECKLIST

Next time you visit a zoo, keep a look out for some of the things mentioned in this book. Use the list below to record what you have seen. Don't worry if you don't see everything. This will depend on where you live and how big the zoo is.

African elephant	fruit bat	penguins
American alligator	gazelle	Père David's deer
ant	giant anteater	pig
aquarium	giant panda	pink pigeon
Arabian oryx	giraffe	polar bear
armadillo	gnu	Przewalski's horse
Asian elephant	goat	pygmy possum
baboon	golden lion tamarin	quetzal
Barbary sheep	gorilla	radiated tortoise
bears	grizzly bear	red fox
birds of prey – hawks	Hawaiian goose (ne-ne)	reptile house
bison	heron	sea otter
black rhino	horse	shark
buffalo	ibis	sheep
bushbaby	jaguar	snake
buzzard	keeper	snakes – boa, python
cages with glass fronts	koala	snow leopard
cheetah	lemur	stork
chimpanzee	leopard	swamp deer
condor	lion	tapir
Congo peafowl	lizard	tarantula
crocodile	llama	tiger
dolphin	loggerhead turtle	toucan
duck-billed platypus	loris	tropical fish
eagles	mandrill	vet
emu	mole rat	volcano rabbit
enclosures with moats	orang-utan	wart-hog
fennec fox	ostrich	white-eared pheasant
flamingo	parrot	white rhino
frog	partula snail	zebra